Karting

ACKNOWLEDGMENTS: The photographs are reproduced through the courtesy of: pp. 5, 24, 25, Barb Pendleton; pp. 6 (top and bottom), 7, 8, 9, Duffy Livingstone; pp. 13, 19, 22, 26, 29, 33, 35, 36, 41, 42 (top and bottom), 43, (top left and top right), 45, 46, 47, the International Kart Federation; pp. 14, 16, 17, 20, 28, 37, 43 (bottom right), Jerry O'Brien, Editor, *World Karting* Magazine; pp. 21, 30, the Daytona International Speedway; p. 32, TNT Kartways; p. 39, Ron Pearson; p. 40, Aurora Speed; p. 43 (bottom left), Mrs. Randy Thompson.

Logos and maps are reproduced through the courtesy of pp. 11 (top), 38 (top), the International Kart Federation, 416 South Covina, California 91724; pp. 11 (bottom), 38 (bottom), the World Karting Association, P.O. Box 2548, North Canton, Ohio 44720.

Go Kart is a registered trademark of the Fox Corporation, Janesville, Wisconsin.

Superwheels & Thrill Sports

KARTING
RACING'S *FAST* LITTLE CARS

ROSEMARY G. WASHINGTON

Lerner Publications Company ▪ Minneapolis, Minnesota

The author wishes to thank the following people for their assistance in the preparation of this book: Ron Black, Pat Davidson, Lynne Gilman, George Kugler, Duffy Livingstone, Jerry O'Brien, Barb Pendleton, Doug Stokes, Terry Traeder. The author also wishes to give special thanks to Sarah Tucker. Editor: Mark Lerner

LIBRARY OF CONGRESS CATALOGING IN PUBLICATION DATA

Washington, Rosemary G.
Karting.

(Superwheels and thrill sports)
SUMMARY: An introduction to karting, including its development, different types of karts and races, professional karting, and champions of the sport.

1. Karting—Juvenile literature. [1. Karting] I. Title. II. Series.

GV1029.5.W35   1980   796.7'6   80-12385
ISBN 0-8225-0435-9   (lib. bdg.)

Manufactured in the United States of America. Published simultaneously in Canada by J. M. Dent & Sons (Canada) Ltd., Don Mills, Ontario.

International Standard Book Number: 0-8225-0435-9
Library of Congress Catalog Card Number: 80-12385

1 2 3 4 5 6 7 8 9 10 90 89 88 87 86 85 84 83 82 81 80

CONTENTS

A champion kart with its driver's sporty helmet on the seat

INTRODUCTION

Tinkering with a lawn mower engine and some metal tubing, Art Ingles was trying to fashion a new toy. As Ingles was a race car builder by trade, it was not surprising that his toy should be something like a car. But Ingles' toy would be smaller than a car, so he called it a "little car." Soon he had fitted four wheels to the metal frame, attached a steering wheel, installed a seat, and adapted a chain to connect the engine and rear wheels.

5

The year is 1957, and Art Ingles is driving around the Rose Bowl parking lot in the first kart ever built.

In late 1957, these karts were the only ones in the world. In almost no time, though, karts became internationally popular.

Ingles, excited by his creation, took the little car to the Rose Bowl, the famous stadium in Pasadena, California. There, in the spacious parking lot, he zipped around on his new toy. The spectators at the Rose Bowl couldn't help but notice Ingles in his tiny car, and they watched in amazement.

Duffy Livingstone, a friend of Ingles, was also excited by the little car. He was so captivated that he quickly built one of his own. Requests for the little cars from friends and Rose Bowl spectators flooded Livingstone, Ingles, and fellow race car maker Lou Borelli. The little-car builders worked fast, and almost overnight a dozen of their products were buzzing around the Rose Bowl. Racing the little machines was instantly popular.

Speaking of the first little cars, Livingstone

said, "We built them for fun, and they just took off from there. We didn't have the foggiest idea of what would happen."

Today Ingles' little car has been developed into a highly sophisticated machine that is raced by all kinds of people. It is easy to see why the popularity of these little cars continues to grow. They offer the same thrills and challenges as big race cars do—and at a fraction of the cost. Because they are inexpensive and easy to maintain, the little cars appeal to people of all ages. Aspiring race car drivers, or those too young to drive cars, can practice their driving skills with the little cars. Fast drivers can race them at dizzying speeds far more safely than they can drive their cars and motorcycles. With their low center of gravity and sturdy construction, the

Karting pioneer Duffy Livingstone drives an early kart.

little cars are easy to handle and control even at speeds as high as 140 miles per hour (mph).

People everywhere now know of the pleasures of the little cars. The tiny machines that began as toys in southern California's parking lots did not remain there long. They spread to all parts of the world, and with them their owners created an entirely new sport, that of kart racing, or karting.

THE EARLY DEVELOPMENT OF KARTING

From his muffler shop in Los Angeles, Duffy Livingstone began manufacturing and selling the little cars. Livingstone, along with partners Bill Rowles and Roy Desbrow, had seen the great demand for the little cars. In almost no time, the mufflers were gone from the shop, and the three partners were spending all their time building more little cars.

All the while Livingstone and his partners were building, selling and promoting their little cars, they were without a name to call them. Lynn Wineland, an advertising man who worked with Livingstone, provided one when he coined the term "Go Kart." ("Zip Kart" and "Dart Kart" were names Wineland considered but rejected.)

The first kart built by Go-Kart Manufacturing

The growing family of little-car drivers now had a name for their machines. All they needed was more room to race. Southern California's parking lots had become congested with karts. There were even complaints that karting was a public menace.

To relieve the problem, Livingstone, Desbrow, Rowles, and Don Boberick built the first kart track. Its name was Go Kart Raceway. And the place chosen for it was Irwindale, California, just outside Los Angeles.

But even before people set aside specific public areas for karting, they wanted to control other safety and technical aspects of the sport. With so many karts around, enthusiasts needed a uniform set of official rules. In response to this need, the world's first karting organization was formed in 1957.

Again, Livingstone played a key role. First called the Go Kart Club of America, the organization later became known as the International Kart Federation (IKF). Today it is

An aerial view of Go Kart Raceway in Irwindale, California. This was the first track built especially for kart racing.

the world's largest governing body for the sport of karting.

The IKF grew very rapidly from the handful of organizers who formed the group in 1957. The list of members increased almost daily, until today the IKF has about 5,500 members, mostly in the United States and Canada.

The IKF's main purpose is to promote safe and fun karting. In competitive karting, the organization determines the rules and regulations for kart equipment and race procedures. On November 21, 1957, the IKF published its first set of rules for competition. These rules have been constantly revised and updated since then. The IKF sanctions, or gives its approval to, only those races that comply with its established guidelines.

The IKF provides other services to its members as well. Always concerned with safety, the organization examines kart-track facilities each year and certifies those that meet its approval. The IKF also publishes a magazine called *Karter News,* which gives members the latest information about kart equipment, manufacturers, race schedules, rule changes, and meetings of the board of directors. The organization even offers its members an accident insurance program.

The success of any organization lies in maintaining open communication between its governing board and its members, and the IKF is no exception. Individual karters elect district representatives, called governors, and members of the national board of directors. This system of communication served all karters well until 1971, when a rift developed. A group of members became dissatisfied with the administration of the IKF and their safety policies. Finally they split away and formed the World Karting Association (WKA).

In order to compete in as many races as possible, many karters belong to both the WKA and the IKF. Usually dual membership does not lead to conflicting interests, for the main objective of the two organizations is the same—to promote safe and fun karting. Indeed, many karters feel that the differences between the WKA and IKF are not great at all. These karters hope that one day the WKA and the IKF will come together and once again form one large karting body.

The International Kart Federation (IKF) logo

The World Karting Association (WKA) logo

THE DIFFERENT TYPES OF KART RACING

Over the years, karting has grown and changed from a "parking lot" recreation to a full-fledged sport. In the process, several types of kart racing have evolved. The different kinds of kart races are run on different kinds of tracks and under different race procedures. The three major types of karting competition are: *sprint racing, road racing,* and *speedway racing.* In addition, other types of karting competition have developed, including *ice racing, Formula Kart Experimental racing,* and *Super Kart racing.*

SPRINT RACING

Sprint racing is the oldest type of kart racing. As its name implies, sprint racing combines high speed and short distances. Sprint races are run on asphalt tracks of three quarters of a mile or less in length. The tracks have several twists and turns, which make driving them a true test of skill.

The kart used in sprint racing resembles Ingles' early kart. A sprint kart can be immediately identified by its "sit-up" driver's position, which is designed for greater control on the twisty sprint courses.

A sprint race includes three separate, shorter races called *heats*. A heat is usually 10 laps around the track. Contestants try to complete the 10 laps of each heat in as little time as possible. Each karter is awarded points on the basis of his or her performance in the individual heats. The final winner of a sprint race is the driver who has the highest total point score from the three heats combined.

Running a fast heat wins a karter more than points. It can also improve the driver's starting position in the next heat. At the start of each heat, the karts line up in two rows. The fastest karts line up in the front, and the slower karts start in the rear. For example, the kart that wins the first heat will start at the front of the *grid*, or lineup, in the second heat. And the kart that finishes last in the second heat must start last in the third heat. Those karts near the front of the grid, of course, have a head start over the karts behind them. For that reason, drivers try to win one of the front positions in as many heats as possible. A driver with a poor showing in one of the early heats not only loses valuable points, but also has to start at the back of the grid in the next heat.

To establish the grid in the first heat of a sprint race, officials run *time trials*. In a time trial, each kart races against the clock. The drivers with the fastest times are awarded front positions for the first heat.

Sprint karts whip around a curve.

Sprint kart drivers remain in *grid* formation until the race begins.

Sprint drivers must maintain their grid positions during the starting procedure for each heat. Most races use *rolling starts,* in which the karters take a warm-up lap or two, slowly traveling behind the lead kart. During this time, all karts must remain in grid formation. If the official starter is satisfied with the speed and formation of the karts as they pass the starting line, they are given the green flag. That signals the start of the race.

From then on, karters may pass each other as they speed toward the finish line.

Although quickness is necessary to win, the many turns and curves in a sprint course prevent karts from reaching maximum speed limits in competition. Drivers must combine strategy and skill with quickness in order to maneuver their karts to a winning finish. Indeed, the thrills of sprint racing attract more people than any other type of kart racing.

Before the race actually begins, sprint karts warm up with a *rolling start*.

The official starter (*right*) waves the green flag and the race is on.

ROAD RACING

Road racing, another type of kart racing, evolved from sprint racing. Early karters, seeking new ways to race their machines, began to run greater distances. Gradually they modified their karts so that they could race for longer periods of time.

The road-racing kart that resulted, also called an *enduro kart*, was quite different from its sprint-racing ancestor. One of the kart's first structural changes involved its fuel-carrying capacity. In order to hold enough fuel to power itself over long distances, the road-racing kart had a large fuel tank mounted onto one or both sides. Other structural changes soon followed. Drivers noticed that at high speeds, wind resistance—caused by air pushing against the driver and the kart—produces *drag*. Drag tends to slow down the vehicle and lower its gas mileage. By exposing less surface area to the wind,

drag can be reduced. Karters discovered that they could reduce wind resistance on their chests and abdominal areas by driving their machines from a "lay-down" position. As a result, drag was reduced and drivers' karts went faster and got better gas mileage. With these changes, the road-racing kart developed a sleek, road-hugging look all its own.

The road race itself also differs from a sprint race. The lengthy course—often a sports car track—has long stretches and a variety of turns. And, instead of judging a race by laps or heats, officials measure the length of a road race by time. Most road races last one hour, though some are only 45 minutes long.

To start a road race, the drivers line up *Grand Prix* style, or side by side, with at least two feet between karts. Unlike sprint karts, road-racing karts take off from *standing*

Road-racing, or enduro, karts have large fuel tanks and long, "lay-down" seats.

starts. This means that drivers take no warm-up laps, although they may start their engines one minute before the race begins. Once the flag drops to signal the start, the vehicles cannot be pushed. After one hour, the racers drive out their final lap to the finish line. The kart that has completed the most laps is the winner. If two or more karts tie for the most laps completed, the first kart to cross the finish line wins the race.

An enduro kart in action at the Indianapolis Speedway

Road races are often run on many of the world's most famous professional sports car tracks. Road-racing karters, young and old, can feel the excitement of speeding down the tracks at Daytona International Speedway, Indianapolis Raceway Park, Ontario Motor Speedway, Watkins Glen Grand Prix, and other motorsport circuits.

The crowded start of an enduro race at the Daytona International Speedway

Dirt sprays out from the tires of this speedway kart.

SPEEDWAY RACING

More commonly known as dirt-track racing, speedway racing was started to provide an inexpensive and fun type of kart racing in areas that did not have asphalt tracks. But the thrill of dirt-track competition is making it one of the more popular forms of karting in all areas of the country.

Speedway races use sprint karts and are run on dirt tracks of a quarter mile or less in length. Like a sprint race, speedway competition consists of three separate heats—two 10-lap heats and one 20-lap heat. The second heat, however, is run from an inverted start. In other words, the drivers who led the first heat have to work their way up from the back of the pack during the second heat. Drivers line up for the third heat according to the number of points they received in the first two heats. As in sprint racing, the overall winner of the speedway event is the driver who has accumulated the most points in all three heats combined.

ICE RACING

It used to be that karters in the northern regions had to put their karts into storage during the snowy, winter months. But several innovative drivers conquered the forbidding terrain and discovered the sport of ice racing.

Both sprint- and road-racing karts can be raced on ice. The basic materials of the machines remain unaltered. The tires, however, are modified to gain traction on ice. Several types of studded tires have been designed to provide adequate grip on the icy track. Some karts have chains wrapped tightly around each tire. Others use a combination of these two types, setting inch-long nails between each link of the chain.

Driving these machines around an oval of ice is a challenge to even the most experienced karter. The races are conducted in the same manner as those on the more traditional asphalt surfaces. Though the top speeds of the karts are reduced, all the thrills of high-speed competition are still there.

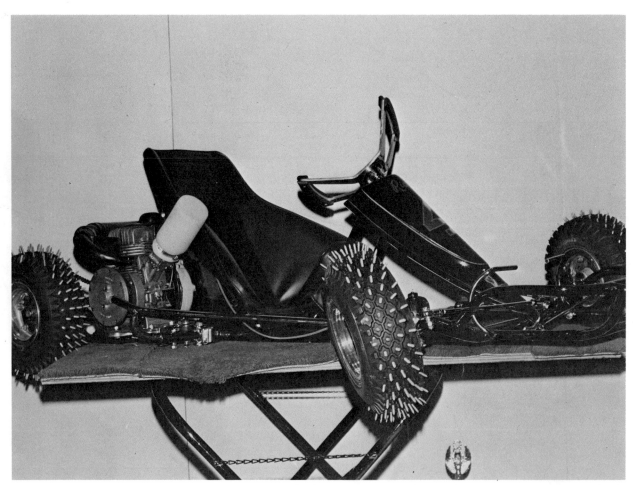

Studded tires enable the kart to race on an ice track.

Drivers hope for traction as they battle each other on a frozen course.

Young drivers waiting to race

KARTING CLASSES

Each of the major types of kart racing—sprint racing, road racing, and speedway racing—has several competition classes. These classes are determined by three factors: the driver's age; the combined weight of the kart and driver; and the engine size and type.

In national competiton, a driver must be at least 9 years old for sprint and speedway racing and 12 years old for road racing. Generally, kart races have several *junior* classes for drivers under 16 and a number of *senior* classes for drivers 16 years and older.

The type of engine in the kart also determines several competition classes. Engine size is the chief factor, but there are other considerations as well. Additional classes separate single engines from double engines, engines with reed valves from those with rotary valves, and *stock-appearing* engines from *modified* engines. Stock-appearing engines come straight from the box and have not been altered at all. Modified engines are allowed some changes. Finally, there are open classes, which place no restrictions on the type of engine used.

A special class included in road racing is the Formula Kart Experimental (FKE) class, which began in 1967. The FKE class is one

A Formula Kart Experimental (FKE) class kart glides down the track.

SUPER KARTS

More than any other type of kart, the Super Kart resembles the big race cars competing at the Indianapolis 500 and in other famous auto races. The Super Kart's powerful 250 cubic-centimeter (cc) engine is actually a motorcycle engine. Like its large race car cousin, but unlike any other type of kart, the Super Kart has a six-speed transmission, which is engaged through a pedal-operated clutch and a hand-operated gearshift.

of only two classes in karting to have karts with bodies. Generally, FKE, or Formula, karts have no limitations except for engine size. As a result, these karts show more variation than other karting classes do. Most Formula karts are hand-built, one-of-a-kind machines. They have metal or fiberglass bodies, and many sport colorful paint jobs.

Super Karts, among the fastest of all karts, resemble race cars in another obvious way: their bodies. Super Kart bodies, like those of the FKE class, are made of fiberglass. In Super Kart bodies, however, drivers are exposed, not enclosed, as they are in the FKE bodies.

Super Karts have powerful 250 cubic-centimeter (cc) engines, six-speed transmissions, pedal-operated clutches, hand-operated gearshifts, and a lot of class.

Super Kart competition came to the United States in 1979. For several years before then, Europeans had been racing this unique type of kart. Perhaps because of their European origin, Super Kart races in the United States are run under the *Fédération Internationale de l'Automobile* (FIA) racing procedure. Under this procedure, Super Kart events are divided into four 15-minute heats. The higher a driver finishes in each heat, the fewer points he or she receives. After all four heats, the driver with the fewest points is the winner.

Since 1979, the World Karting Association has taken the lead in sponsoring Super Kart events. It sanctions races on both the oval road-racing tracks and the twisting sprint-racing courses.

Super Karts competing at the Daytona International Speedway

KARTING SAFETY

As karting has grown, so has its emphasis on safety. Today, all drivers and karts entering officially sanctioned events must comply with the rules established by the karting organizations. In case of injury, drivers also carry accident insurance, which is paid for through their IKF or WKA membership dues.

THE PRE-RACE TECHNICAL INSPECTION

One of karting's most important safety precautions is the pre-race technical inspection. The purpose of this inspection is to insure that the karts operate safely while racing. A kart is eligible to compete only after meeting all of the safety standards.

Before the karts are allowed out onto the track, they must report to a special inspection area. There karts are checked for faulty construction and defective equipment that could become a hazard to the driver or other drivers during a race. For example, the inspectors make sure that the tires are free of flaws, that the brakes perform well, and that the throttle closes automatically upon release.

Inspectors also check the overall construction of each kart to see that it gives the driver the greatest possible protection. The driver's compartment of an enduro, sprint, or Super Kart must have side rails or other side support. No part of the driver can extend beyond the length or width of a kart. Safety regulations also require that any part of the kart extending beyond the body that could puncture or injure other competitors must be fitted with a safety guard.

The FKE vehicle must include other special protective devices for its driver, who is enclosed in a metal or fiberglass body. Fire walls must separate the driver's compartment from the engine. Seat belts, a fire extinguisher, and a special roll bar for the driver, which must be positioned directly above his or her helmet, are also required.

Even with its emphasis on safety, karting has its share of accidents as these unlucky drivers found out.

SAFETY IN COMPETITION

The strong emphasis on safety does not end with the pre-race technical inspection. Safety is of prime importance during the race, too. The race tracks must provide an ambulance, a first-aid kit, and a qualified medical person at every racing event to handle a possible emergency. The track must also set up protective barriers along the raceway to prevent bystanders from being struck by a kart.

Drivers, too, have to follow certain safety standards during the race. Any driver in violation of the safety rules is immediately disqualified. At the start of each race, each entry must have on hand a dry-powder fire extinguisher as a precaution against fire on the track. Competitors are required to wear protective gear to prevent burns and other injury. This gear includes a helmet, goggles or face shield, long pants, and a leather or heavy vinyl jacket. FKE drivers, who are enclosed by the body of their kart, must wear

A driver wears protective clothing, including helmet, face shield, long pants, and jacket.

clothes made of fire-resistant material. Many karters also wear ear plugs to guard against hearing loss from loud engine noise.

Safe driving methods and competition techniques also reduce the possibility of accidents during a race. Drivers are licensed and, in addition, have to demonstrate their driving skills to the satisfaction of race officials before they are allowed to compete.

During the actual race, drivers must give consideration to their competitors. Bumping and blocking another kart is not allowed. Drivers use a system of arm signals to warn each other of impending danger on the track caused by mechanical failure, a pileup, or loss of control. When a driver is being overtaken by a faster kart, he or she must raise one arm to indicate the safest side for passing.

Flag signals by officials along the raceway also warn drivers of changes in the conditions of the track. A yellow flag tells karters to slow down and hold position because the track is partially blocked. A red flag indicates that the track is unsafe for racing and that all karts must stop immediately. A black flag waved at a particular driver may mean mechanical problems or disqualification for bad driving practices. A racer who has been "black flagged" must finish the lap at reduced speed and stop at the race official for instruction before resuming competition.

THE POST-RACE INSPECTION

The outcome of a kart race is not official immediately after the race is over. Before any winners can be announced, the drivers must pass a post-race inspection. The purpose of this inspection is to check the legality of the karts and to make sure that the karts and their drivers meet the class weight requirements. The post-race inspection guarantees that the race was run fairly.

Immediately after their final laps, all par-

A flagman explains flag signals. Before racing, all drivers must know what each flag signal means.

ticipants must drive their karts directly to the inspection area. They are not allowed to stop because they could possibly make changes on their vehicles at that time.

In the first step of a post-race inspection, a kart and its driver are weighed together on a large scale. The racer is weighed in the clothes that had been worn during the race, including helmet, shoes, and jacket. The combined weight is set for each class before the race. Karters who know before the start of the race that they may have light karts often carry *ballast,* or heavy weights, during the race so that they will be sure to pass the

A driver and kart about to be weighed during the post-race inspection

post-race inspection. Any karter who is below the class weight is disqualified.

Next, the karts are checked to see that they do not exceed the maximum size set for each race. Each type of competition kart must meet length, width, height, wheelbase, and tread-width specifications. Those that do not meet these standards are disqualified.

Finally, the engines are inspected thoroughly. They are checked for illegal additions or modifications on standard parts. When a kart passes the engine test, as well as the other post-race inspection tests, it is eligible for any awards it may have won on the track.

The 1979 WKA Winter Enduro Nationals at the Daytona International Speedway. With 946 karters competing, this was the biggest karting event in history.

CHAMPIONSHIPS

The Daytona International Speedway hosted kart racing's biggest event ever—the 1979 WKA Winter Enduro Nationals. At Daytona, 946 karters from around the world competed in 19 different classes. The WKA Winter Enduro Nationals are held every December at Daytona Beach, Florida. This race is one of the four major events of the kart-racing year. The others are the WKA Winter Olympics in Barnesville, Georgia, every March, and the IKF Road-Racing Grand Nationals and the IKF Sprint Grand Nationals, which are both run annually at different tracks during the summer. The winners of these amateur races receive handsome trophies and valuable prizes, as well as the prestige that comes with being a karting champion.

While the grand national championship races highlight the kart-racing season, national championship events are nearly as prestigious. Among them are the Central

Sprint Winternationals and the Eastern Sprint Winternationals, both of which are sanctioned by the IKF. Just below the national level of competition is the divisional level. Regional races are run in each of the nine WKA divisions in the United States, and championship races in each of the ten IKF divisions across the United States and Canada. In addition to the grand national, national, and divisional races, there are hundreds of local races held throughout the year. At these races, drivers new to karting, or those who cannot afford to travel to the big races, compete against each other. The IKF and WKA sanction local races and award points to the top finishers. At the end of the kart-racing season, both karting organizations name the year's hi-point champion in each class.

Major kart races are also held outside the United States and Canada. Karters from all over the world travel every year to the Hong Kong International Karting Prix. In Europe, the World Championships of karting take place every summer. Drivers from South America, Japan, Canada, and the United

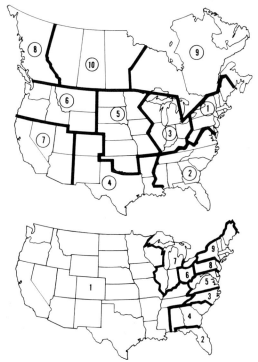

The divisions of the International Kart Federation (top) and the World Karting Association (bottom)

States compete against the finest European drivers. Because a country may send only five drivers to the World Championships, this international event has the strongest competition of them all.

Lake Speed drives to victory in the 1978 World Championships at Le Mans, France.

CHAMPIONS OF KARTING

In 1978, Lake Speed proved what many people had believed for a long time—that he was the best kart driver in the world. Lake did this by winning the karting World Championships at Le Mans, France. Before his international victory at Le Mans, Lake had won nearly every important race in the United States at least once. Three times he has claimed a sprint-racing national championship title in the B-Open class, and, in 1975, he was the C-Open class champion in both sprint and road racing. All tolled, the kart shop owner from Jackson, Mississippi, who has been racing since 1961, has won over 20 national championships.

Lynn Haddock, Lake's friend and mechanic at Le Mans, has won perhaps more titles than any driver in karting. Lynn started racing in 1958, when he was eight years old. Since then, he has captured over 20 WKA titles and almost as many IKF titles in both sprint and road racing. In 1977, Lynn proved his

Karting champions Lynn Haddock (*far left*) and Lake Speed (*second from right*) inspect karts during the 1976 World Championships at Hagen, West Germany.

versatility as a driver by winning the Reed Open and B-Limited class national championships in *both* the sprint and enduro competition. The Chattanooga Choo Choo, as this engine builder from Chattanooga, Tennessee, is known, gained international recognition with his victory in the 125cc class at the 1975 Hong Kong International Karting Prix.

Often called the "Queen of Champions," Kathey Hartman has shown that success in karting may come to women as well as to men. Kathey is one of the most successful drivers in karting history. Competing in a sport dominated by men has not prevented Kathey from winning 15 national and 3 grand national titles. In fact, no other driver has won two grand national championships in a row, as Kathey did in 1971 and 1972. While compiling an impressive list of sprint-racing victories, Kathey has been most outstanding in the enduro competition. Kathey would quickly admit that her achievements in karting must be shared with her husband, John, chief of Hartman Engineering, which introduced the first lay-down enduro kart in 1963.

Kathey Hartman, the "Queen of Champions"

Kyle Adkins, the "California Flash"

Other top karters who deserve mention along with Speed, Haddock, and Hartman include grand national champions Kyle Adkins, Bob Pruitt, Gary Emmick, Linda Emmick (Gary's wife), and Howard Combee, who has also won the Hong Kong International Karting Prix. Veteran drivers Mark Dismore, Dave Knapp, and Terry Traeder have won karting honors for many years, while bright young stars such as Texas state champion in Junior I and II classes Adam Thompson and 1979 Barnesville Winter Olympics champion Denise Johnston promise to be big names in karting for years to come.

Linda Emmick and a young fan

Top drivers Howard Combee (*left*), a Hong Kong International Karting Prix winner, and Mark Dismore (*right*), winner of many national championships

Bright young stars in karting's future—Adam Thompson *(left)* and Denise Johnston *(right)*

PROFESSIONAL KARTING

Karting reached a milestone in 1974 when the first professional race was held. The race took place after much promoting and organizing by experienced karters such as Lake Speed and Lynn Haddock. They felt that karting had to advance beyond its amateur status in order to provide better competition for the best drivers in the sport. A pro class would set the drivers who saw karting as a daily activity apart from those who raced karts as a weekend hobby. Speed and other advocates of professional karting believed that a pro class would also benefit karters with little competitive experience. Without a pro class, the same people would win almost every race, and new drivers would become frustrated by having to compete against the "hot shoes," or top drivers. In the long run, this would not be good for karting, as drivers would become discouraged and eventually leave the sport.

So the pro class was born. Quickly, it developed its own set of rules, as well as another name—the *Expert* class. Professional karting was set up as an open class with only a few restrictions. Engines were required to have a 6.1 cubic-inch displacement, and kart and driver were required to weigh at least 300 pounds at the end of the race. A few years after the first rules were set, restrictions were placed on the drivers. Drivers who won three grand national titles in their classes in amateur racing were to be considered experts, and drivers who won money in pro events would not be permitted to race in amateur competition.

Dave Knapp won the first pro race, earning most of the $1,000 purse that the Memphis, Tennessee, track offered. The following year, Lynn Haddock was acclaimed Pro Champion by winning the $3,000 First Annual Pro Race of Champions, run at the TNT Kartways in

Dave Knapp, winner of the first professional kart race

Quincy, Illinois. In 1977, Kyle Adkins became the first driver to win two pro races in succession when he defeated the best in karting at the U.S. Open in Barnesville, Georgia, and at the Second Annual Pro Race of Champions at Quincy, Illinois.

Five years after the first professional kart race, the Professional Karting Association (PKA) was formed by Terry Traeder of Quincy, Illinois, and Jim Reed of Edison, California. Its goal was to promote the pro class and to serve as a membership body for

the best drivers in karting. In 1979, the PKA, with the Bridgestone Tire Company as sponsor, organized the first professional series. It was called the PKA Bridgestone National Pro Series. The series consisted of three events. Lynn Haddock won the first, held at Quincy, Illinois. And he also won the second, run in Jacksonville, Florida. Each race earned Lynn $2,500. The final event of the 1979 pro series took place in Medford, Oregon, with Rick Gifford of Norco, California, driving his way to victory and $2,500. The PKA national high-point champion, or the driver with the best overall performance in the three races,

Terry Traeder waves two checks as he celebrates a pro-race victory.

was Haddock. As PKA national high-point champion, he received $3,000.

Professional karting is the fastest growing of all karting classes, and with its growth more and richer PKA events will surely follow.

CONCLUSION

To those who participate in karting and who know how exciting and challenging it is, the sport's tremendous growth is not surprising. And with the ever-growing popularity of karting, the future can hold nothing but more races and greater competition for the sport's new and old drivers—all of whom will continue having fun and thrills with racing's fast little cars.

Superwheels & Thrill Sports

Lerner Publications Company
241 First Avenue North, Minneapolis, Minnesota 55401